OCT - - 2019

ALTERNATOR
BOOKS™

SURVIVING
A WORLD WAR II
PRISON CAMP

LOUIS
ZAMPERINI

MATT DOEDEN

Lerner Publications ◆ Minneapolis

Lerner Publications Company
A division of Lerner Publishing Group, Inc.
241 First Avenue North
Minneapolis, MN 55401 USA

For reading levels and more information, look up this title at www.lernerbooks.com.

Library of Congress Cataloging-in-Publication Data

Names: Doeden, Matt, author.
Title: Surviving a World War II prison camp : Louis Zamperini / Matt Doeden.
Other titles: Louis Zamperini
Description: Minneapolis : Lerner Publications, [2018] | Series: They survived
    (Alternator Books) | Includes bibliographical references and index.
Identifiers: LCCN 2018004440 (print) | LCCN 2018013928 (ebook) | ISBN
    9781541525634 (eb pdf) | ISBN 9781541523548 (lb : alk. paper)
Subjects: LCSH: World War, 1939–1945—Prisoners and prisons, Japanese—Juvenile
    literature. | Zamperini, Louis, 1917–2014—Juvenile literature. | Prisoners of
    war—United States—Juvenile literature. | Bomber pilots—United States—
    Biography—Juvenile literature. | Survival—Juvenile literature.
Classification: LCC D805.J3 (ebook) | LCC D805.J3 D64 2018 (print) |
    DDC 940.54/7252092 [B]—dc23

LC record available at https://lccn.loc.gov/2018004440

Manufactured in the United States of America
1-44439-34686-7/5/2018

CONTENTS

INTRODUCTION

DANGER ABOVE DANGER BELOW

The sound filled Louis Zamperini with hope. It started as a low, distant rumble. Zamperini heard it from the two small life rafts he shared with Russell Allen Phillips and Francis McNamara. The men had been adrift for twenty-seven days since their plane had crashed into the Pacific Ocean. They were **dehydrated** and starving. Soon Zamperini saw a small speck against the blue sky. It was an airplane!

Zamperini fired a **flare** into the sky. He grabbed a packet of colored dye and dumped it into the water. The dye spread out across the blue of the ocean, marking the raft's spot for the airplane's crew.

The plane continued on its path. Then, just as the men began to believe that it hadn't spotted them, it turned around. It was coming back!

Zamperini wept with joy. He took off his shirt and waved it in the air. The plane, a bomber, drew low.

Then the bomber opened fire. It was the middle of World War II (1939–1945), and the bomber was not a US plane. It belonged to Japan—the enemy.

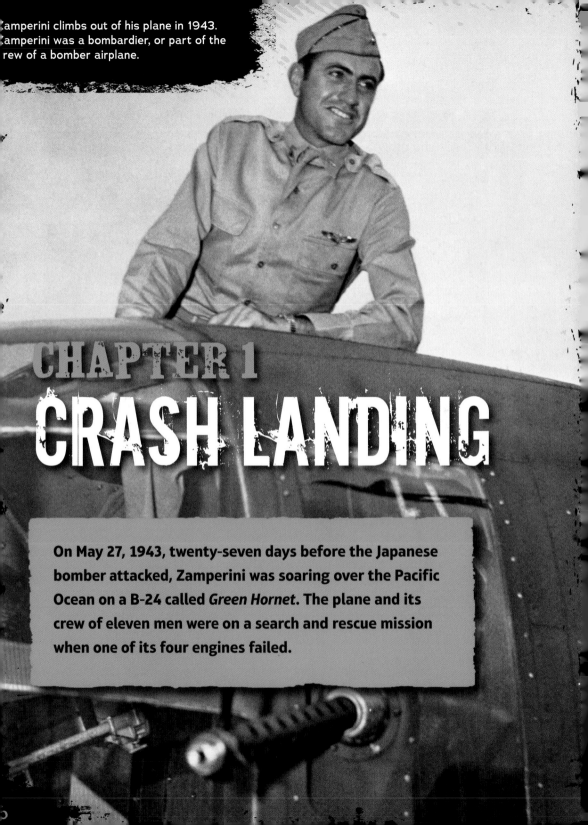

Zamperini climbs out of his plane in 1943. Zamperini was a bombardier, or part of the crew of a bomber airplane.

CHAPTER 1
CRASH LANDING

On May 27, 1943, twenty-seven days before the Japanese bomber attacked, Zamperini was soaring over the Pacific Ocean on a B-24 called *Green Hornet*. The plane and its crew of eleven men were on a search and rescue mission when one of its four engines failed.

As the plane's pilots struggled to hold the plane steady, another engine failed and the plane fell into a spiral. "Prepare to crash," Phillips called out.

The impact ripped the B-24 to shreds. Water rushed into the plane as it began to sink. Zamperini was trapped in a tangle of wires. As the water and darkness swallowed him, something struck his head. In the moments before he passed out, he was sure that he was going to die.

Zamperini examines damage to an airplane made by a Japanese explosive shell during a 1943 mission.

A World War II pilot participates in a training exercise. Zamperini likely completed similar training before his mission.

Zamperini awoke, choking on water and gasoline. Somehow, he'd come free of the wires, but he was running out of time. Zamperini kicked his way through a window. Once he was clear of the sinking plane, he pulled a cord on his inflatable life vest. A canister of compressed air filled the vest, pulling Zamperini to the surface. He gasped for air as he emerged and then vomited all the salt water he had swallowed.

The scene was a nightmare. Pieces of the shattered plane littered the ocean surface, and huge slicks of oil and fuel spread out in every direction.

A voice called out. It was Phillips, clinging to a piece of **debris**. McNamara was with him. Zamperini started to swim for one of the plane's life rafts, but it was floating away too quickly. Then he spotted a long cord trailing behind it. He grabbed the cord and pulled the raft back. The three men climbed inside. They spotted another raft nearby and paddled to it.

Zamperini, Phillips, and McNamara survived in a life raft similar to this one. The men in this raft are completing tests of survival equipment.

They looked for more survivors, but there were none. The three men were adrift on the open sea, with almost no food or water. They had survived the crash. But their struggle was just beginning.

A scene from the 2014 movie *Unbroken*, about Zamperini's World War II experience, shows the men adrift in the Pacific Ocean.

OLYMPIC STAR

Zamperini was famous before he ever joined the Army Air Forces. In 1936, at the age of nineteen, Zamperini qualified for the US Olympic team in the 5,000-meter (3.1-mile) race. He was the youngest distance runner to ever make the team.

The Olympics were held in Germany, which was controlled by Adolf Hitler and the Nazi Party. Hitler was watching as Zamperini ran in the finals of his event. Zamperini fell back in the early laps of the race, but he ran the final lap in a blistering fifty-six seconds.

Impressed, the German dictator asked to meet Zamperini. The two shook hands, and Hitler congratulated him. "Ahh, you're the boy with the fast finish," the dictator said.

Zamperini (*center*) poses with other Olympic hopefuls at the Olympic tryouts in New York on July 13, 1936.

Japan controlled much of the surrounding land and water during World War II.

CHAPTER 2
27 DAYS

The ocean currents carried the rafts west—toward Japanese-held territory. The odds of seeing a friendly plane grew dimmer.

It was a constant struggle for survival. Sharks shadowed the raft. The men gathered rainwater when they could. But it often went days without raining, and they suffered from dehydration. During the day, the hot sun beat down on the men, while they huddled for warmth at night. Salt covered their bodies. It ate away at their skin, leaving painful sores.

Around the fourteenth day at sea, an **albatross** landed on Zamperini's head. He grabbed it and killed it. The men had eaten so little in recent days that they ate the vile-tasting bird raw. Inside the bird's stomach were several small fish, which Zamperini used as bait to catch a larger fish.

An albatross soars over the ocean. Zamperini caught and ate several of these seabirds during his time at sea.

SURVIVAL GEAR

Zamperini, Phillips, and McNamara survived on two life rafts that were just 6 feet (1.8 m) by 2 feet (0.6 m). The rafts were stocked with an emergency kit that included a few high-calorie chocolate bars, water tins, a flare gun, dye for dropping into the water to mark the raft's position, a brass signaling mirror, and a patching kit. The emergency kit also contained fishing line, fishhooks, a screwdriver, and pliers.

A World War II emergency kit similar to Zamperini's contains a flare gun, food, water, and a patching kit.

As the days passed, the men grew even more desperate for food. So Zamperini tried for larger game. He waited for a small shark to swim near the boat, and then he grabbed it by its tail, threw it into the raft, and killed it. Zamperini had been taught that the liver was the only part of a shark that was good for eating, so he cut it out, and all three men ate their fill.

Then, on their twenty-seventh day at sea, the Japanese bomber opened fire on them. The three men dove into the water and swam under the rafts as bullets rained down on them. The bomber passed, and the shooting stopped. The men surfaced.

In a scene from *Unbroken*, the men flag down what they think is a rescue plane.

A Japanese plane made several passes, raining bullets on the men and damaging their rafts.

The bomber turned to make another pass. Below, a different kind of danger lurked. Two hungry sharks, which had trailed the men for weeks, headed toward them. Zamperini helped Phillips and McNamara back into the raft just as the bomber returned. Zamperini dove as the bomber fired again. Phillips and McNamara lay in the raft, too weak to return to the water.

As Zamperini hid under the raft, one of the sharks came at him. Zamperini dodged its jaws as it attacked. When the shark came back again, he punched it in the nose.

Zamperini climbed onto the raft as the bomber passed and returned to the water when it came back, fighting off the sharks with his fists and feet. The bomber made four more passes. Then, when Zamperini's strength was almost gone, the bomber finally rose into the sky and did not return.

Somehow, the three men had survived. But the news was grim. One raft was destroyed, and the other was littered with bullet holes. If it sank, there would be no fighting off the sharks.

Zamperini did the only thing he could. He found the raft's patching kit and got to work.

A scene from *Unbroken* shows the men after the Japanese bomber attack.

CHAPTER 3
FROM BAD TO WORSE

In the weeks before the attack, Zamperini and Phillips had tried to remain positive. They spoke of home and dreamed of rescue. Zamperini would describe his mother's cooking, and they imagined feasting together, all while their bodies wasted away. McNamara, however, was distant and withdrawn. He expressed little hope of survival.

Just a few days after the Japanese bomber attacked, McNamara faded away. He died sometime around the thirtieth day, and Zamperini and Phillips gave him a burial at sea.

As the weeks stretched on, Zamperini and Phillips grew weaker and weaker. Then, on the forty-sixth day, they spotted land—the Marshall Islands, a chain of islands between Hawaii and the Philippines. A day later, after surviving a night filled with **typhoon** winds and waves, they paddled toward it.

Japan had several air and naval bases in the Marshall Islands. During the war, US forces attacked these bases and gained control of the islands.

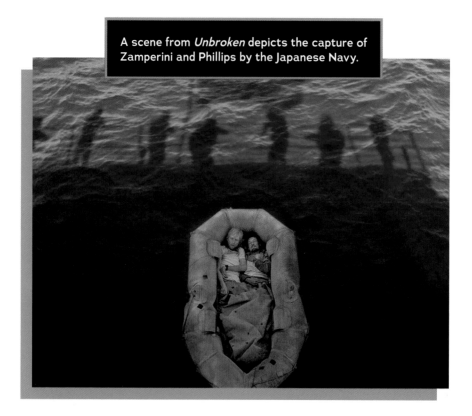

A scene from *Unbroken* depicts the capture of Zamperini and Phillips by the Japanese Navy.

As they drew near, a boat appeared. It pulled alongside their battered raft. Faces stared down at them—Japanese faces.

The sailors brought them aboard, and soon the Japanese moved the prisoners to a second boat. "These are American fliers," said a Japanese officer. "Treat them gently."

The sailors treated their new prisoners well. They cared for their wounds and fed them all they could eat. After a few days, the Japanese moved the pair to a prisoner-of-war (POW) camp on a nearby island.

This began a new ordeal. The Japanese sailors had been kind, but the prison guards were not. They stripped and beat the prisoners. They **interrogated** them again and again. Zamperini was sure he and the others would be killed.

Many prisoners in Japanese POW camps were put to work in mines and factories. They were given very little food and were beaten if they did not follow instructions.

One of the Japanese guards recognized Zamperini from his days as an Olympic runner, which may have saved his life. The Japanese moved Zamperini and Phillips to a POW camp near Tokyo, Japan, and separated them. Zamperini was held prisoner for more than two years. He and his fellow prisoners were starved, beaten, and forced into hard labor. The conditions were terrible, and they suffered from disease such as **dysentery**. The **warden** of the prison, Mutsuhiro Watanabe, took a special interest in Zamperini. He singled out the former track star for extra punishment and terror. At times, Zamperini barely clung to life. His fellow prisoners sneaked him extra food and helped keep him alive.

Actor Miyavi plays prison warden Mutsuhiro Watanabe in the movie *Unbroken*.

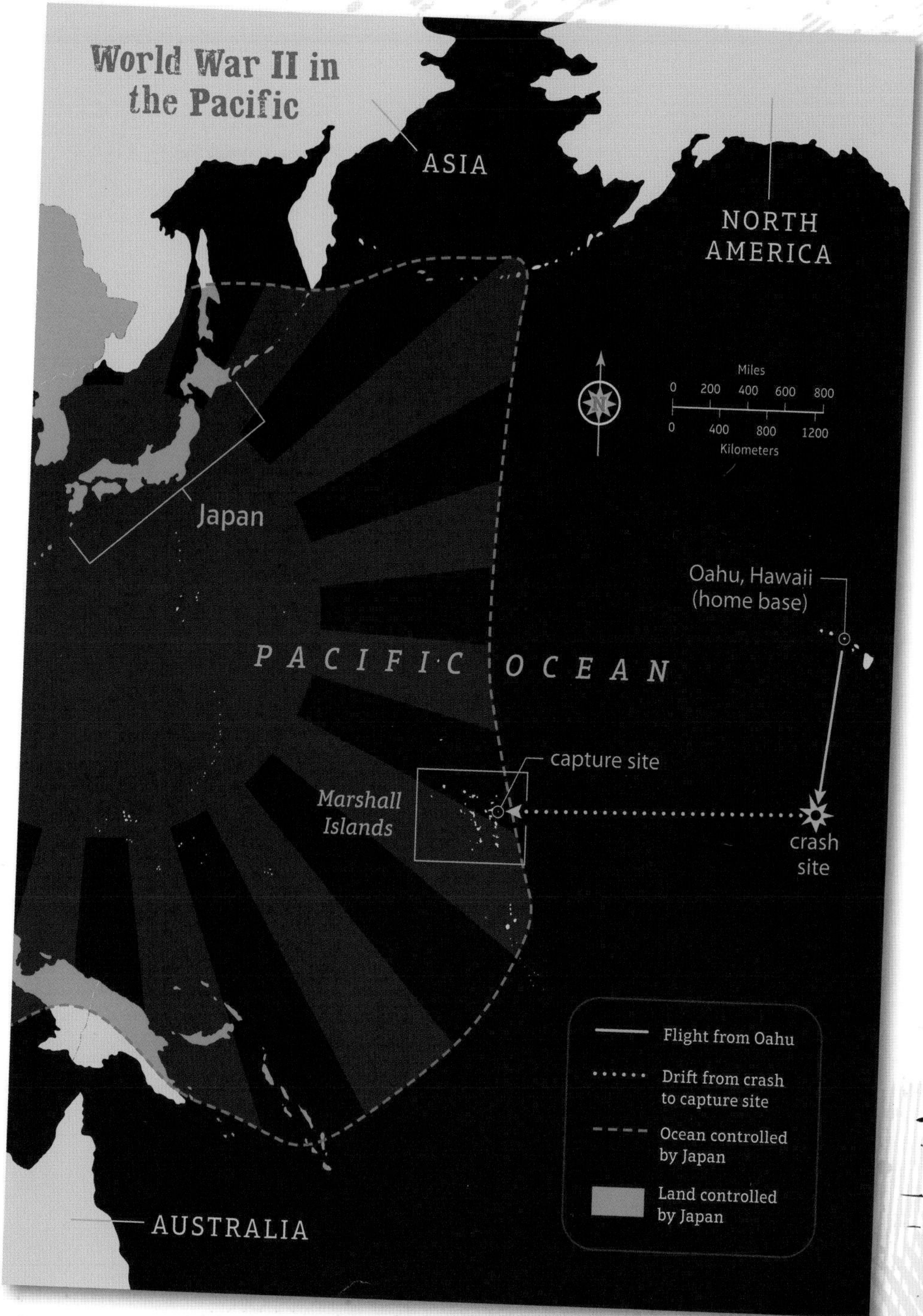
World War II in the Pacific
ASIA
NORTH AMERICA
Japan
PACIFIC OCEAN
Oahu, Hawaii (home base)
capture site
Marshall Islands
crash site
AUSTRALIA
Miles
0 200 400 600 800
0 400 800 1200
Kilometers
N
Flight from Oahu
Drift from crash to capture site
Ocean controlled by Japan
Land controlled by Japan

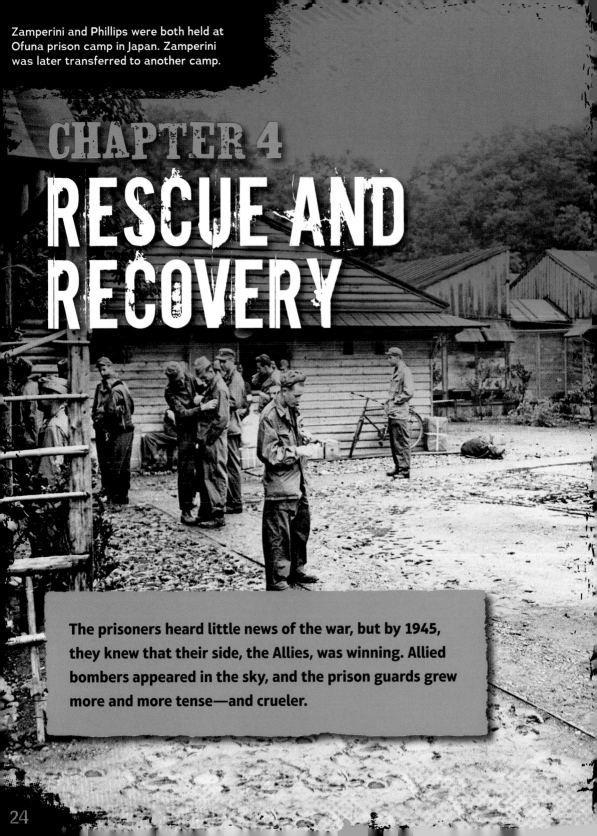

Zamperini and Phillips were both held at Ofuna prison camp in Japan. Zamperini was later transferred to another camp.

CHAPTER 4
RESCUE AND RECOVERY

The prisoners heard little news of the war, but by 1945, they knew that their side, the Allies, was winning. Allied bombers appeared in the sky, and the prison guards grew more and more tense—and crueler.

By August 15, 1945, Zamperini was in bad shape. His fellow prisoners didn't know how much longer he could survive. But that day, everything changed. The guards told the prisoners that the war was over.

In the following weeks, US planes appeared in the sky. But this time, they weren't dropping bombs. They were dropping supplies for the prisoners.

Japan formally surrendered on September 2, 1945, bringing World War II to an end. During a ceremony marking the surrender, US planes flew in formation over Japan.

Zamperini and the others in his camp were finally rescued on September 5, 1945. He boarded a train, and then he took a ship back home to the United States. He had been believed dead and was welcomed home as a hero. So was Phillips, who also made it home alive.

Zamperini stands with his mother, who made cookies to welcome him home in 1945.

SURVIVAL STORY

SURVIVAL

RESILIENCE

REDEMPTION

UNBROKEN

THE UNBELIEVABLE TRUE STORY

CHRISTMAS

Zamperini's story made news upon his return to the United States but was soon forgotten. That changed in 2010 when author Laura Hillenbrand published a biography detailing his struggle for survival. Her book, *Unbroken: A World War II Story of Survival, Resilience, and Redemption*, spent four years on the *New York Times* best-seller list.

In 2014 Hillenbrand's book was adapted into a feature film, *Unbroken*. The American Film Institute named it one of the top ten films of the year.

In 1950 Zamperini visited Sugamo Prison, where Japanese war criminals were held. Zamperini faced the prison guards who had once tormented him and who were now imprisoned for their war crimes.

For the first time in more than two years, Zamperini was safe. But he struggled to return to his former life. He fell into fits of rage, and nightmares haunted him. He abused alcohol, and he dreamed of revenge against those who had hurt him.

Zamperini believed that he had to face his tormentors. So in 1950, he returned to Japan. He stood face-to-face with some of the men who had beaten and humiliated him, and he forgave them. Then he was finally ready to move on with his life.

SURVIVING DEADLY SITUATIONS

Zamperini and Phillips survived against seemingly impossible odds. How did they do it? What lessons can we learn from their ordeal?

1. Stay positive. Always work on surviving. Never give up. Zamperini and Phillips kept a positive outlook, which may be part of the reason they survived and McNamara did not.

2. Use supplies carefully. When food and water are scarce, use only enough to get by, so that supplies last as long as possible.

3. Seize opportunities. Even though sharks were a constant danger to Zamperini, they also presented an opportunity. He caught one, providing much-needed food.

4. Rely on others. Zamperini's story is proof that in a survival situation, others can be your greatest asset. Zamperini helped Phillips when he was hurt in the crash. Later, other prisoners helped keep Zamperini alive. Neither Zamperini nor Phillips would have survived alone.

5. Take chances. Know that the possibility of rescue always makes a gamble worthwhile.

6. Never give up. No matter how bad things got at sea or in the prison camps, Zamperini kept working to survive.

SOURCE NOTES

7 Laura Hillenbrand, *Unbroken* (New York: Delacorte, 2014), 123.

11 Hillenbrand, 36.

20 Hillenbrand, 179.

GLOSSARY

albatross: a large seabird

debris: pieces of wreckage

dehydrated: lacking water in the body

dysentery: a disease of the digestive system that causes vomiting and diarrhea

flare: a signaling device that is fired into the air and burns very brightly

interrogated: asked questions forcefully

typhoon: a very strong tropical storm found in the Pacific or Indian Oceans

warden: the person in charge of a prison

FURTHER INFORMATION

Hillenbrand, Laura. *Unbroken: An Olympian's Journey from Airman to Castaway to Captive*. New York: Delacorte, 2014.

HowStuffWorks: "How to Survive a Shipwreck"
https://adventure.howstuffworks.com/how-to-survive-a-shipwreck1.htm

McNab, Chris. *Survival at Sea*. Broomall, PA: Mason Crest, 2015.

Mooney, Carla. *Surviving in Wild Waters*. Minneapolis: Lerner Publications, 2014.

Olson, Tod. *Lost in the Pacific, 1942: Not a Drop to Drink*. New York: Scholastic, 2016.

Survival Expert: Survival at Sea
http://www.survival-expert.com/Adrift_at_Sea.htm

Unbroken: Louis Zamperini
http://www.louiszamperini.net/

World War II for Kids
http://www.ducksters.com/history/world_war_ii/

INDEX

PHOTO ACKNOWLEDGMENTS

Image credits: Sakarin Sawasdinaka/Shutterstock.com, p. 1; Roger Viollet/Getty Images, pp. 4–5; Bettmann/Getty Images, p. 6; National Archives (342-FH-3A-42819), p. 7; National Archives (80-G-K-13767), p. 8; National Archives (80-G-42014), p. 9; Photo 12/Alamy Stock Photo, pp. 10, 15, 17, 20, 22, 27; AP Photo, pp. 11, 24; Keystone-France/Gamma-Keystone/Getty Images, pp. 12, 26; Wayne Lynch/All Canada Photos/Getty Images, p. 13; National Archives (342-FH-3A12880-69837AC), p. 14; Time Life Pictures/The LIFE Picture Collection/Getty Images, p. 16; Greg Vaughn/Alamy Stock Photo, p. 18; National Archives (127-gr-20-136-72428_001-ac), p. 19; John Swope Testamentary Trust/Corbis Historical/Getty Images, p. 21; Laura Westlund/Independent Picture Service, p. 23; National Archives (80-G-421130), p. 25; Kyodo via AP Images, p. 28. Design elements: Miloje/Shutterstock.com; Redshinestudio/Shutterstock.com; sl_photo/Shutterstock.com; Khvost/Shutterstock; Milan M/Shutterstock.com; foxie/Shutterstock.

Cover: Bettmann/Getty Images (portrait); National Archives (342-FH-3A03305-71865AC) (background).